Charlie & Wilbur's

DINOSAUR MAZES

Written and illustrated by

Patrick Merrell

Sterling Publishing Co., Inc.
New York

Dedicated to:

Lloyd
Mazer

Nancy
Shack

2 4 6 8 10 9 7 5 3 1

Published by Sterling Publishing Co., Inc.
387 Park Avenue South, New York, NY 10016
© 2007 by Patrick Merrell
Book design by Patrick Merrell
Distributed in Canada by Sterling Publishing
c/o Canadian Manda Group, 165 Dufferin Street,
Toronto, Ontario, Canada M6K 3H6
Distributed in the United Kingdom by GMC Distribution Services,
Castle Place, 166 High Street, Lewes, East Sussex, England BN7 1XU
Distributed in Australia by Capricorn Link (Australia) Pty. Ltd.
P.O. Box 704, Windsor, NSW 2756, Australia

Printed in China

Sterling ISBN-13: 978-1-4027-3800-5
ISBN-10: 1-4027-3800-5

For information about custom editions, special sales, premium and
corporate purchases, please contact Sterling Special Sales
Department at 800-805-5489 or specialsales@sterlingpub.com.

Dinosaurs roamed the earth 200 million years ago.

But they weren't alone.

They shared their neighborhoods
with lizards, snakes, tortoises,
small furry mammals, insects,
flying reptiles, birds, fish, and
in the small town of Rockville...

...a crocodile named Charlie
and a turtle named Wilbur.

Welcome to
ROCKVILLE
Founded 2,000,007 B.C.

I LOVE MAZES

One day, Wilbur went over to watch TV at Charlie's house. "Bad news," Charlie said. "The TV's broken."

"Broken?!" Wilbur gasped. "But we'll miss our favorite show!"

"I thought we could solve the mazes in my new DINO DIGEST instead," Charlie said.

Charlie and Wilbur loved mazes.

"Ooh! Lookie! An IGUANODON!" Charlie exclaimed as he turned to the first maze. "One of my favorites!"

"It looks just like Mrs. Abromowitz down the street," Wilbur said. They both chuckled.

The APATOSAURUS maze was too big to fit on one page.

DINO FACT:
APATOSAURUS is often called BRONTOSAURUS, but the name APATOSAURUS was given to it first.

Start

It had to share the next page with a SAUROLOPHUS maze.

The last maze in the magazine went through three SCELIDOSAURS!

Start

Keep going!

One more!

End!!

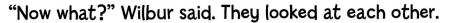

"Now what?" Wilbur said. They looked at each other.

"Let's draw a maze and tape it on the TV!" Charlie said.

"Yeah, then there will be something good on TV!" Wilbur said.
They both chuckled.

Next they decided to draw mazes on Charlie's dirt floor.
Just as they were finishing there was a loud crash outside.
"Yikes! What was that?" Charlie said. He hustled through his maze
to the front door.

Wilbur scampered through his maze to the side door.

"Egad!" Charlie said when they got outside. "It's Rex!"

Charlie's neighbor, a TYRANNOSAURUS, had knocked over a large pile of logs in the front yard.

"What a klutz!" Wilbur said. "His name should be Wrecks instead of Rex." They both chuckled.

Note: Travel ON the logs!

But Rex's wreck had created a fun maze for the two of them to solve. "Last one through is a rotten ZEPHYROSAURUS egg!" Wilbur said as he raced along the tops of the logs.

DINO FACT: *TYRANNOSAURUS was one of the largest meat eaters ever. A full-grown person might be the height of a tyrannosaur's knee.*

When they got to the spot where the logs had been piled, Charlie found something.

"It's my last month's issue of DINO DIGEST!" he said. "I was wondering why I never got it."

He immediately turned to the mazes in the back. The first was a SPINOSAURUS maze.

"Hey, this PROTOCERATOPS maze is the only other one in the magazine!" Charlie grumbled.

"Looks like we're going to have to find some more mazes on our own," Wilbur said.

"Let's go get my bike!" Charlie said after they'd finished both mazes.

Charlie and Wilbur hustled around to the storage cave in Charlie's backyard.

"I wish Fred would hurry up and finish eating the lawn," Charlie said. "It looks so messy like this."

"He's very slow," Wilbur agreed. "Even for a CAMARASAURUS."

There were five keyholes on the cave door, but only one of them actually unlocked it. The others were fakes! Charlie had drawn a maze on the door to remind himself which keyhole was the right one.

Important: The working keyhole is the FIFTH one the maze route comes to!

"This cave is just too big!" Wilbur grumbled. "And filled with too many boxes!"

"You're right," Charlie said. "I can't see my bike anywhere."

"Climb up on top of my head," Charlie said.

"Ah, that's better," Wilbur said after he had done so. "There it is!" he exclaimed, pointing across the cave.

"Where should we go?" Charlie asked.

"How about Duckbill Hill?" Wilbur suggested. "We haven't been up there for weeks."

"A+ idea, Wilbur!" Charlie said. Wilbur hopped in the front basket of the bike and off they went.

End!

Duckbill Hill looked out over the whole valley.

Charlie pulled out his binoculars and peered through them. "Look, two PLESIOSAURS in the river," he said. "I think they're heading over to check out the volcano."

"Watch out, PLESIOSAURS!" Wilbur yelled as he took a look through Charlie's binoculars. "The volcano is erupting!"

Lava started flowing down the side of the mountain.

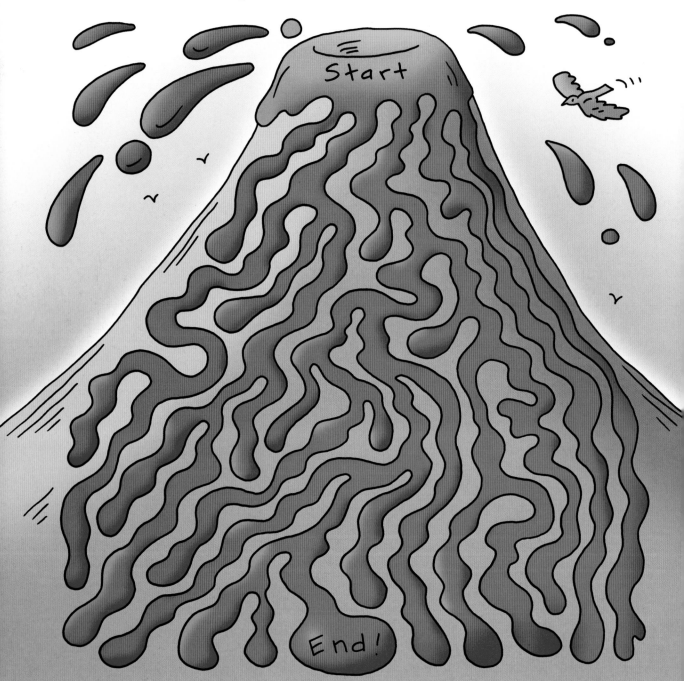

"Hmm, looks like the lava has trapped that VELOCIRAPTOR," Wilbur said.

Charlie took a look. "Yeah, but he'll be able to hop across those rocks to safety."

Start

End

As Charlie and Wilbur coasted down the hill, they saw a small pack of STEGOSAURS.

"Must have been a late night," Wilbur remarked. "Look at them dragging their tails."

"I bet I can figure out whose tail made which line in the dirt," Charlie boasted.

DINO FACT: A STEGOSAURUS brain was the size of a walnut.

As they approached a lone SALTOPUS,
Charlie pulled his bike over.
"What's up, Sally?" he said.
"I'm trying to catch up to my friends,"
she said. "But they're so far ahead."

"Hop on," Charlie said. "I'll push."
"Whee! Look, no hands!" Sally said
as they raced down the road.

29

After they'd gotten Sally back to her pals, they stopped to rest. Charlie was worn out.

Wilbur saw an ANKYLOSAURUS and decided to draw a maze in his sketchbook.

"Heh heh. Nice maze!" Charlie said. "Let me try one."
He took Wilbur's sketchbook and drew a maze with a
DRYOSAURUS in it.

As they started for home, they ran into their neighbor, a TRICERATOPS.

"Hey, Mrs. Horn!" Charlie called out. "Could you lead us through the earthquake field?" They weren't sure which way to go.

Start

"Duck, Wilbur! PTERODACTYLS!" Charlie yelled after getting through the earthquake field. Wilbur ducked inside his shell but then peeked out to follow their paths.

DINO FACT: PTERODACTYLS weren't dinosaurs. They were flying reptiles.

Charlie had to swerve to avoid a MUSSAURUS baby. It was no bigger than a young kitten.

The little fellow was playing hide-and-seek with his pals.

"Yay! Almost home!" Charlie said as he pedaled onto their street. "To celebrate," Wilbur said, "I'm going to draw a maze using two of the longest dinosaurs ever: BAROSAURUS and DIPLODOCUS!"

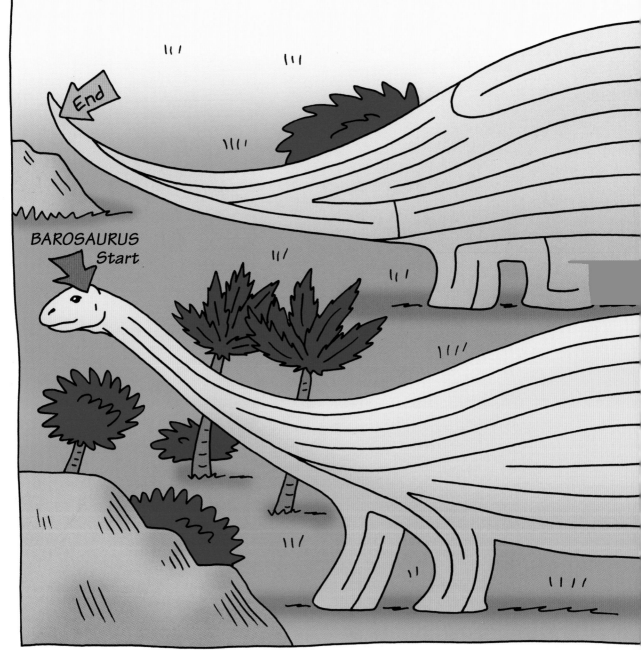

He pulled out his sketchbook and had the mazes all done by the time they pulled up to Charlie's house.

DIPLODOCUS Start

End

"Whew, that was some day!" Wilbur said when they were inside.
"I'm so hungry I could eat an ULTRASAURUS!" Charlie said. "Put something good on the TV while I get us some dinner, will ya?" he added. And that's just what Wilbur did.

THE ANSWERS

PAGE 5

PAGE 6-7

PAGE 8

PAGE 9

PAGE 10

PAGE 11

PAGE 12-13

PAGE 14

PAGE 15

PAGE 16

PAGE 17

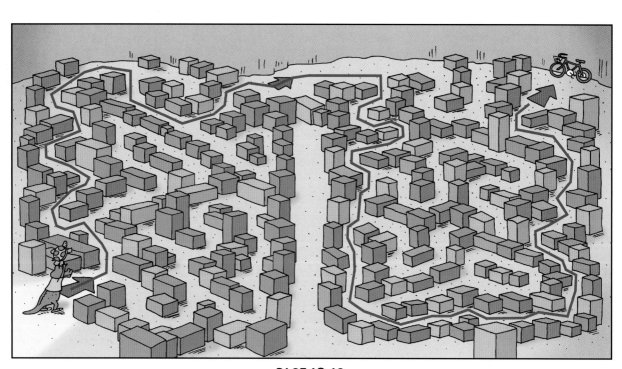

PAGE 18-19

PAGE 20-21

PAGE 22-23

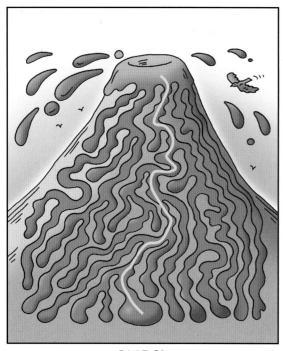

PAGE 24

PAGE 25

PAGE 26

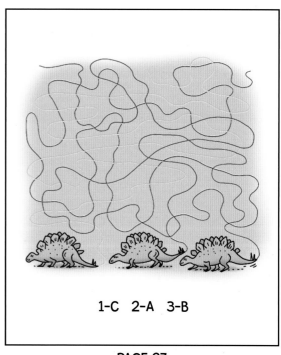

1-C   2-A   3-B

PAGE 27

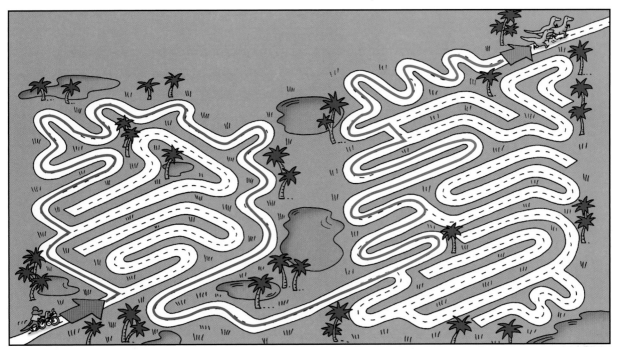

PAGE 28-29

PAGE 30

PAGE 31

PAGE 32-33

1-A 2-B 3-C

PAGE 34

PAGE 35

PAGE 36-37

PAGE 38

DINO FUN FACTS

MEGALOSAURUS, which means "giant lizard," was the first dinosaur to be named, in 1824.

MAIASAURA was the first dinosaur in space! In 1985, MAIASAURA bone and egg fragments were taken up in NASA's space shuttle.

SAUROPOSEIDON, perhaps the tallest dinosaur ever, would have been able to see over a six-story building with its incredibly long neck.

COMPSOGNATHUS, one of the smallest dinosaurs, was no bigger than a chicken.

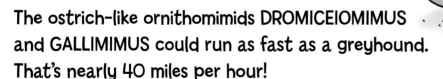

The ostrich-like ornithomimids DROMICEIOMIMUS and GALLIMIMUS could run as fast as a greyhound. That's nearly 40 miles per hour!